With thanks to:

Bob and our family for their support
and encouragement as I write
Spiritual Books for Children

And to Maggie Margolis for sharing with
me her childhood memories of the city

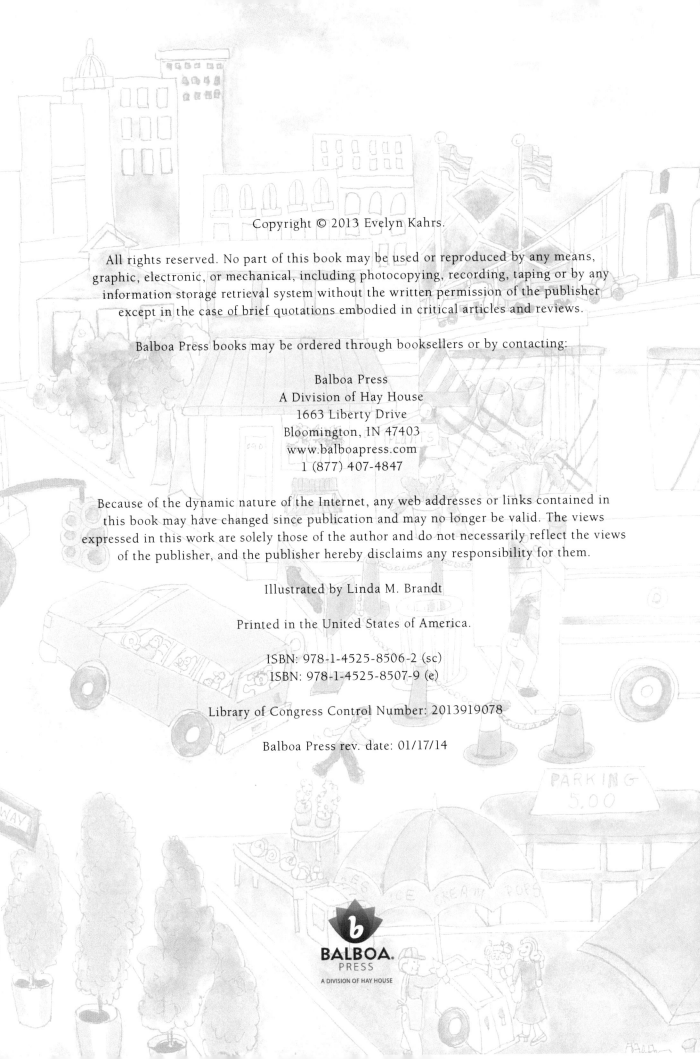

Balboa Press books may be ordered through booksellers or by contacting:

Balboa Press
A Division of Hay House
1663 Liberty Drive
Bloomington, IN 47403
www.balboapress.com
1 (877) 407-4847

Illustrated by Linda M. Brandt

Printed in the United States of America.

ISBN: 978-1-4525-8506-2 (sc)
ISBN: 978-1-4525-8507-9 (e)

Library of Congress Control Number: 2013919078

Balboa Press rev. date: 01/17/14

BALBOA.
PRESS
A DIVISION OF HAY HOUSE

I CAN FIND
GOD IN MY CITY

. . . .

EVELYN KAHRS

. . . .

ILLUSTRATED BY LINDA M. BRANDT

Can I find God in my city? Yes, I can!
I can find God ...

In stores filled with things for us all to buy
In buildings that seem to go up to the sky

In parks in the
spring, and the
summer, and fall

With my friends
playing soccer,
baseball and all

On ice rinks in winter,
where we are all skating

In the zoo where seals and monkeys are waiting

In apartments and houses
where people reside

In dogs being walked with their people beside

In subways
that run so far
underground

In cars, taxis and buses moving people around

Everyone going somewhere
or else coming home
And trains going everywhere
under its dome

In museums filled with
paintings, sculptures and all

In others with dinosaurs ever so tall

In firemen who fight
the fires in walls

In garbage
collectors in
trucks filled
with trash

In vendors who
work from their
little food carts

Selling hotdogs or apples or maybe some tarts

In the very tall building that
towers high over all

I look down from the top and
my city looks small

In theatres where
artists perform
day and night

In the Nutcracker Ballet,
a wondrous holiday sight

In the Little Red Light House
almost hidden from sight

On the big bridge above it filled
with cars day and night

On boats in the river and planes in the sky

In the Statue that's holding
her light up so high

Wherever I look, wherever I go
Up toward the sky and
way down below
Where can I find God in my city?

God is found in every spot.
There is no spot where God is not! ***
I can find God EVERYWHERE!

***from the song "There is no Spot Where
God is Not" by Karen Drucker and Maggie Cole.
Turn the page for the music and words.

There Is No Spot

Words: Maggie Cole & Karen Drucker
Music: John Hoy & Karen Drucker

is no spot where God is not. There is no spot where

God is not. God is me. God is you.

God's in ev-ery-thing_ we do.__ There is no spot oh where God is

not.

There

D.S. al Coda

Made in the USA
Columbia, SC
22 January 2022

54625660R00022